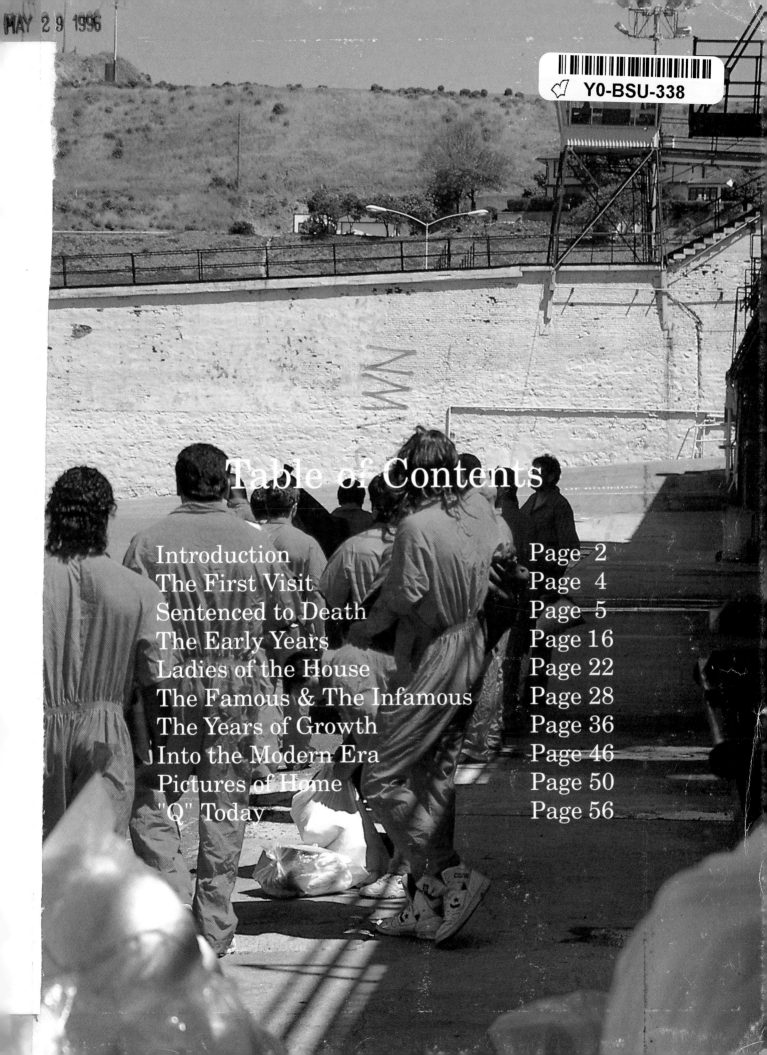

Table of Contents

Richard A. Nelson
Associate Warden, San Quentin State Prison,
Unit II (Death Row)
President, San Quentin Museum Association

In 1986, a group of San Quentin employees, retired staff, historians, educators and local residents joined together and organized the San Quentin Museum Association. They joined together to preserve the history and the artifacts. But, perhaps more important, to tell the true story of San Quentin. A story not just seen by the staff or inmates or portrayed in books and film. San Quentin through the years has changed in many different directions but so has our society. Every change in the laws, morals, dress, economics and politics have a direct effect upon the lives "inside the walls" of the prison.

This pictorial collection is the first of hopefully many volumes in which we can share a part of San Quentin's history. This volume welcomes you with photographs and narratives, into San Quentin Inside The Walls as it is today.

A special thanks to Jeff Craemer my friend for his counsel, dedication and especially his research.

This book is dedicated to all of the men and women, both staff and inmates, who have served time at "Q".

San Quentin Inside The Walls

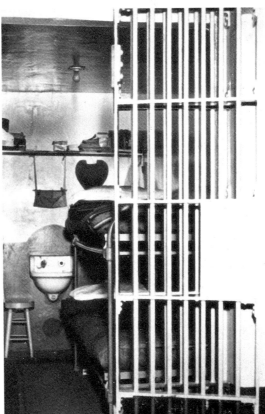

Nancy Ann Nichols, Text
James Delahunty & Nancy Ann Nichols, Editing
Alan H. Nichols, Contemporary Photographs

SAN QUENTIN PRESS ✣ SAN QUENTIN

Dr. Leo Stanley

The First Visit . . . A trip to San Quentin in earlier years is recounted by Dr. Leo Stanley. Hired as an assistant resident physician in 1913 he was promoted to Chief Physician the following year and held that position until his retirement in 1951. He graduated from what would become Stanford Medical School. He and his wife lived on the prison grounds. Mrs. Stanley, who developed tuberculosis prior to Dr. Stanley's employment at San Quentin, died a few years later. Her illness was a major reason for Dr. Stanley being in the forefront of treating the disease. At San Quentin he introduced new concepts such as open-air sunrooms for his tubercular patients.

The following is an account of Dr. Stanley's first visit to San Quentin:

"They got Repsold. His body was found stuck in the mud in Corte Madera Creek half a mile above the Horse Post."

That was the news imparted by Bill Magill, the driver of the long horse drawn bus awaiting the ten o'clock steam train at Greenbrae Station.

On the mile ride to San Quentin, Magill told in detail more of what had happened. That was my first trip to San Quentin Prison, a place in which I was destined to spend 38 years. I had come this cold February morning in 1913 as a young doctor, just out of medical college, to inquire about the position of assistant to the Resident Physician

In the long open air bus with parallel seats were two deputy sheriffs each with a handcuffed prisoner whom they were taking to the penitentiary. I wondered what these men, both young, might have been sent up for and what their sentences might be. Alongside me were several women, possibly wives, mothers or sweethearts who were going over on visiting day. And too, there was a Salvation Army officer loaded down with a wicker basket. No doubt filled with gifts for his men.

Next to me was a dentist, Dr. Tom Barr from San Rafael. He visited the prison twice a month to care for the teeth of the two thousand or more inmates there at the time. And on board were several guards who had come in on the train after a days holiday in San Francisco. The bus stopped at the Horse Post on the edge of the prison grounds, so called because nearby was a horse saddled, bridled, and ready to be mounted

to give chase to any convict who might attempt to take to the hills.

"Yes, he's in the morgue. They found him over there on that mud flat. He thought he could cross the creek and the swamp. But he got stuck in the mud. The tide came up and drowned him", volunteered the Horse Post Guard the information of Magill for his fellow prison officers and other passengers aboard the bus.

At the prison I learned more of the details. Repsold, the Perfumed Burglar, had been sent up from San Francisco for "porch climbing." He had selected likely residences in the Pacific Avenue fashionable area. While the occupants slept, he gained entrance by fire escape or unlocked window. In stocking feet he silently looted the premises carrying away valuable jewelry, money and treasures. The victims of the burglaries arising in the morning found their valuables gone. But remaining in the room was the scent of a very rare and exotic perfume

It was not a difficult task for the police to trace this perfume to a young man named Repsold. His father owned a large wine company named after him. His mother was a very charming French woman. He was an only child with every advantage money could supply. It's a mystery as to just why he persisted in scenting himself with unusual perfumes.

At San Quentin he became a trusty. One cold winter night he managed to get outside the prison walls. He pulled the electric fuses throwing the institution into darkness. In this manner he headed up to Corte Madera Creek and to his ultimate frightful and agonizing death...

Sentenced to death . . .

Capital Punishment was part of the California Criminal Practices Act of 1851. It was reincorporated into the California Penal Code on February 14, 1872. Prior to 1893, sheriffs of the individual counties were responsible for handling executions. Official records indicate that in 1893 San Quentin was designated as the site for executions to be held. A total of 409 people have been executed at San Quentin including 4 women. Anton Vital (#14964), born in Smyrna and described as a "Hindu," was the first person on Death Row. However, his sentence was commuted to life imprisonment and he died in Napa, California in 1901. Jose Gabriel (#15173), a 60 year old native Californian, who was hanged on March 3, 1893, was the first official state execution at San Quentin.

The following is taken from a copy of a prison log discovered in an old San Quentin storage room. The information has not been officially verified. While it mentions hangings, it could be that the executions were done for Marin County (location of San Quentin), for neighboring counties (ie. San Francisco), or for offenses committed while at San Quentin.

No. 15173 / Jose Gabriel
Murder, First Degree
San Diego
Received: December 19, 1892
Executed: March 23, 1893
Hanged
Pronounced Dead
Weight: 140 lbs.
Height: 5' 3 1/8"
Age: 60

Jose Gabriel, convicted of the murder of Augusta Geyser on October 16, 1892.

May 14, 1873:
Very cloudy and cold this morning, the coldest since May 1. Three prisoners arrived on the afternoon boat. Captain Lee B. Mathews returned to his post on the evening boat. ***Dennis, the famous stage robber was hanged today.***
Whole number of prisoners, 934.

May 15, 1873:
After the rain, weather cleared off and is very cold this morning, wind from the North West. Two prisoners discharged this morning by expiration of sentence. One prisoner arrived on the 11 o'clock boat. Oscar Cohn was pardoned today by his excellency Governor Newton Booth. ***Mortimer was hanged today.***
Whole number of prisoners, 932.

July 25, 1873:
Calm, clear morning and very warm. Wind in the West. ***Russell hanged.*** This is the hottest day of the season, temperature 102°.
Whole number of prisoners, 925.

October 3, 1873:
Cool, blustering morning and foggy and cloudy. Wind from the North West. One prisoner arrived today on the 11 a.m. boat. ***Captain Jack Schonchin, Black Jim and Boston Charley were hanged today.*** This was the first triple execution in the history of the prison.
Whole number of prisoners, 929.

January 23, 1874:
Clear morning and a very white frost but very little wind in the North East. Judge William Dennis died in the hospital last night, the remains were sent to Stockton. ***Marlin was hanged today and his head was jerked while he was being executed. Evidently the drop was too long.***
Whole number of prisoners, 939.

5

"I never presided over the execution of an innocent person, although several of the ninety whose death I ordered . . . claimed innocence right up to the last minute."

Warden Clinton Duffy

What is it like to be present at a hanging? Writers have described it as being "unpleasant" to "hellish." Dr. Leo Stanley, whose job as Chief Physician was to pronounce the inmate dead, provides an "opportunity to experience a hanging" with the following words from his journal:

July 28, 1927 –
Another condemned man in today. Eight here now. Wish they wouldn't come in so fast.

August 2, 1927 –
Hate to have to see those condemned men. But if they need medical attention, it must be given them. Nasal polyps. This chap probably has many good qualities – certainly has nerve. Doesn't complain when those polyps are being removed. Peculiar mentality, though. Said that after September the twenty-third the polyps won't bother him any more. Has rather full neck – grewsome to think about the noose tightening about it. Probably deserves what is coming to him, though.

August 16, 1927 –
Condemned man in again for treatment. Breathes better. More polyps to be removed. Has good physique. Examination shows no disease. In a few weeks he'll be dead. Polyps come away all right. A little pain only. Some bleeding. Requested that no newspapers be stuffed in his head at autopsy. Newspapers have caused him too much trouble already, he said. Wanted sawdust. Don't know what his crime is. Killed somebody, of course.

September 1, 1927 –
Condemned men out for exercise. Get one hour a day in sunshine. Wish they wouldn't call to me as I pass. Dislike getting to know them - makes it so much harder to officiate at the execution. Man with polyps walks briskly with head down. Wonder what he thinks? It's to be a double execution on the twenty-third. Other fellow is a Mexican.

September 21, 1927, 1:30 p.m. –
There go the condemned men to the barber shop - it'll be the last shave and bath for the two of them. Would think they would try to commit suicide. Seldom do though. We all know we can't escape death, but these two know the exact time.

5:00 p.m. –
The condemned men are being taken to the death chamber. The other prisoners shouldn't stare through their wickets at them. Morbid curiosity. Unless the governor intervenes, they'll go day after tomorrow.

September 22, 1927, 9:00 a.m. –
The guard just came in for a small bottle of whiskey for the condemned men. Said they were bearing up all right. Maybe the guards take a nip, too. Don't blame them. Certainly unpleasant to be on death watch.

4:00 p.m. –
Governor just wired a commutation to life imprisonment for the Mexican. Said he killed his common-law wife while drunk. Had been good worker and circumstances were mitigating. Will come down tonight. Other poor devil will die though.

8:00 p.m. –
Seems to me that lodge night always comes on Thursday before execution. Will go. Many of the men ask when the next hanging is to take place. Some want to come. Do not care to talk about it, so change the subject.

September 23, 1927, 7:00 a.m. –
Will make ward rounds early, for execution takes place at ten.

8:00 a.m. –
Guard comes for more whiskey. Says trying time for condemned man comes when he changes from prison clothes to black suit. A little drink helps at this time. He paced the floor most of night. Slept only a little.

8:30 a.m. –
Can't get impending execution off my mind. Will finish ward rounds, though.

9:00 a.m. –
The body will not be claimed. Has a wife in the east. Guess she has been sufficiently disgraced. The medical school will be glad to get it. Law says to hold for twenty-four hours. There comes one of those professors now with his assistants.

9:15 a.m. –
Those professors seem heartless, but they don't know the man. It's impersonal to them and they need the material for their classes. Will send them down to the morgue until it is over.

9:30 a.m. –
Everything is still. All men are locked up. No machinery running. Certainly is quiet. Impending doom. Only thirty minutes to live.

9:40 a.m. –
Warden wants me to go up with him. His first execution. The witnesses, about fifty, are coming through the gate. Must be twenty guards with them. Pleasant thoughts for the other condemned men who see them come in. My assistant looks pale and is trying to conceal his nervousness.

9:45 a.m. –
This toilet room certainly is warm, or is it just tension? Why should this effect one's kidneys? All right, its time to go. I'll take off my white coat. Yes, have small bottle of smelling salts in my pocket. Stethascope is all right. My watch is correct - 9:45. Haven't forgotten anything.

9:50 a.m. –
This long climb of three flights of steps taxes one's lung capacity. Will stop at the top of the stairs to get my breath.

9:53 a.m. –
The witnesses and the guards are waiting just outside the execution room. There's that red-headed reporter and the sheriff. And over there is the black coffin. Will soon be filled.

9:54 a.m. –

My watch has same time as Turnkey's. None of these officials look any too happy.

9:56 a.m. –

There go the three guards into the little enclosure. They cut the strings. One string releases the trap. That bucket of water and cup might be useful.

9:57 a.m. –

There is the Warden. Looks distressed. The iron doors are opening. In come the witnesses. The mountain out there looks peaceful. The jute mill is stopped.

9:58 a.m. –

Only two minutes. This thing should be pulled off on time. One Warden always came up fifteen minutes after ten. No use to wait. Too much tension.

9:59 a.m. –

The Warden and guards are going into the death chamber. One has a leather strap to buckle around the legs - the black cap, too.

9:59 $^1/_2$ a.m. –

No noise. Someone breathing hard. Pale faces. Shuffling feet.

10:00 a.m. –

They're going up the thirteen steps - going fast, too. The priest chanting. Footsteps on the trap. Won't look at the man - never do. Nasal polyps. Second-hand of watch moving. Strap buckling around ankles.

10:01 a.m. –

Tripping of trap. Black figure hurled into space. No rebound. Chest bared. Hangman's knot. Swollen veins, neck. Step-ladder. No movement of body. Stethascope. Watch. Heart beat 90.

10:01 $^1/_2$ a.m. –

1...2...3...4...5...6...7...8...9...10...11...12 – heart regular. Is everything getting black? No - am not fainting. Broken neck. Wish this was over. 50...51...52...53...54...55. Vagus nerve blocked. 85...86...87...88.

10:02 a.m. –

My respiration rapid? Calm down. Skin is getting moist. 30...31...32...33. Maybe deserved it. That black suit - lifeless, too. 57...58...59...60. Heart rate twice normal - horse without driver 79...80...81...82.

10:02 $^1/_2$ a.m. –

Dull thud. Someone has fainted. My assistant will care for him. Bucket of water. 27...28...29...30...31. My fifty-third hanging. God, I wish there were no more of these. 40...41...42...43...44. Usually takes eleven minutes - only two gone. 75...76...77...78...79.

10:03 a.m. –

1...2...3...4...5. No irregularity. Assistant recording heartbeats. Kymograph - newspaper would mention it though. "Don't fill my head with newspapers - they caused me enough trouble." 45....46...47...48...49...50. A girl with a red rose. Dive brawl, I guess. San Pedro, sailor. 75...76...77...78...79...80.

10:03 $^1/_2$ a.m. –

Hand aching - will hold on to black coat. Heart doesn't slow up much yet. 15 . . . 16 . . . 17 . .

. 18 . . . 19. Good physique. Laborer. Take on fat in condemned cells. No exercise. 40...41...42...43...44 - this half-minute is long 72...73...74.

10:04 a.m. –

Guess this is necessary. Only the poor get the rope. Leopold and Leob. Millions. 32...33...34...35. Blue denim slippers. 45...46...47. Hangman walking about. Good fellow. Who would want his job? 65...66...67...68.

10:04 $^1/_2$ a.m. –

Why that pain in my heart? Stooped position, I guess. 10...11...12...13. Head almost touches scaffold. Had drop of only five feet, eight inches. 41...42...43. Heart not quite so forceful. 58...59...60.

10:05 a.m. –

Only one in a hundred murderers hang. Usually get fair trial. 30...31...32...33...34. Will be a few minutes yet ...49...50...51...52...

10:06 a.m. –

Lose consciousness when they come to end of rope? Yes? No? When the black cap fell off that colored fellow's face three years ago I saw his face writhe - surely was conscious. Pulled the cap on again. 44...45...46

10:06 $^1/_2$ a.m.

Sacco and Vanzetti. Electric chair. Nevada State Prison, Carson City, lethal gas. 38...39...40.

10:07 a.m. –

This ladder is uncomfortable. Will shift to other foot. 20...21...22...23... Heart sounds are weaker and slowing up. 35...36...37.

10:07 $^1/_2$ a.m. –

What if he should come to life after I have pronounced him dead? Sometimes hearts stop in ten minutes. Stepladder hurts my knee. Will shift to other foot. 27.....28.....29.

10:09 a.m. –

Heart beats slowing down. 2.......3.......4.......5....... Oxygen supply shut off. 11.......12.......13.......Will not be long now. 18.......19.......20.

10:09 $^1/_2$ a.m. –

1.......2.......3 slight irregularity. Crowd restless. Someone whispering. 16.......17.......18.

10:10 a.m. –

Can hardly hear heartbeats. Will shift stethascope. 11...............12. Wouldn't want to pronounce him dead while his heart still beats. 15 ....16.

10:10 $^1/_2$ a.m. –

Only an occasional beat.

10:11 a.m.

Have heard no sound for past half-minute.

10:11 $^1/_2$ a.m. –

Surely must be dead. Don't want to make any mistakes. Will be five minutes though before crowd gets out and he is cut down.

10:12 a.m. –

No sound.

10:12 $^1/_2$ a.m. –

Dead.

Cells on Death Row.

Entrance to Death Row.

Exterior view of the gas chamber.

Execution Procedures for Gas Chamber

1. Received from County. Automatic appeal to California Supreme Court started.
2. 90 days after reception – social, psychological, psychiatric study completed.
3. One (1) year or more – judgement affirmed (or reversed) by California Supreme Court.
4. If AFFIRMED – execution date set by committing court – 60 to 90 days away from signing of execution order.
5. Prior to execution:
   a. 90 days prior - Appoint three (3) psychiatrists.
   b. 30 days prior - Psychiatric report, custodial, warden and religious evaluations.
   c. 7 days prior - Psychiatric report.
   d. 1 day prior - Last visit with family in the morning. Man moved to holding cell around 5:00 p.m. Meal as chosen by inmate served at 6:00 p.m. Warden, Chaplain of choice, or other officials may visit during evening. Kept under direct observation all night.

   Women are brought up from the California Institution for Women, Corona, and are housed in the holding cell on this day, under supervision of women matrons.
6. Execution Day:
   7:00 a.m. - Breakfast served.
   8:00 a.m. - Chamber is readied; Chaplain and Medical officer arrive.
   9:35 a.m. - Cyanide pellets fastened in place.
   9:45 a.m. - Warden and staff arrive
   9:50 a.m. - 12 witnesses and newsmen admitted to Witness Room.
   10:00 a.m. - Warden signals; man placed in chair; chamber sealed; well under chair filled with sulphuric acid; cyanide lowered into acid.
   10:06 - 10:14 a.m. - Doctors pronounce person dead.
   10:15 a.m. - Witnesses leave, Warden leaves, acid and gas neutralized and removed from chamber and Warden notifies Sacramento.
   11:00 a.m. - Remains removed to local mortuary or to mortuary of family's choice.

There is no state executioner. A five (5) man team, under a supervising officer, operate the chamber, transport the condemned man, and carry out the overnight watch.

JWLP:fd / 4-26-71

The electric chair has never been used at San Quentin because it was considered inhumane and degrading to the inmate. The gas chamber came into use in 1938 and the last hanging was done in 1942. Prisoners sentenced to be hanged overlapped in the introduction of the gas chamber. Today, on execution days, all inmates are confined to their cells until after the morning execution is completed.

Since 1893, according to prison records, the ethnic breakdown of the executed prisoners is as follows:

White	281
Black	57
Latino	34
Other	37
Total	409

The prison records show that most of the 409 people executed had committed an act of murder because of some romantic problem. Either wives or girlfriends were killed or somebody whom the murderer felt was interfering with the relationship. The second largest group executed had killed while committing a robbery. A small number were killers for hire and mentally disturbed multiple murderers. No one was described as either a hero, a political prisoner, or someone who died for a cause.

Warden Clinton Duffy

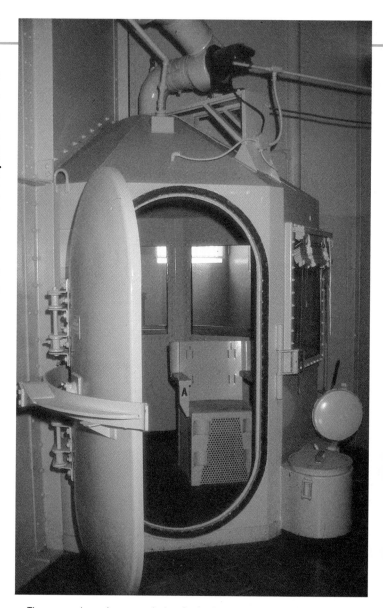

The gas chamber contains 2 chairs so that two people may be executed at the same time.

From 1940 to 1952, Clinton Duffy was warden of San Quentin. Although Warden Duffy was a very vocal and active advocate of abolishing the death penalty, he did say, "I never presided over the execution of an innocent person, although several of the ninety whose death I ordered...claimed innocence right up to the last minute. The evidence against these people was so convincing that I seriously doubt miscarriages of justice."

There was one particular inmate of whom Warden Duffy openly spoke. Caryl Chessman was the author of his own book titled, "CELL 2455, DEATH ROW." The popular press printed a tremendous amount of material on Caryl Chessman. One revealing comment made by Warden Duffy about Chessman was, "I knew [him] well, and if he

is ever recognized as a martyr, it will be a travesty. Chessman was one of the most dangerous men I ever knew, for he combined the brains of a savant with the morals of a degenerate . . . He charmed almost every outsider he met during his twelve years on death row, but he hated them all. . . . In death row he was a tough prisoner to handle – mean, demanding, contemptuous, arrogant, and defiant . . . Chessman could build a very plausible case on an utterly fictitious premise . . . he found it comparatively easy to sell himself to those who never saw him at his worst."

Caryl Chessman was executed on May 2, 1960. Although many executions have been carried out for crimes of murder, Caryl Chessman was one of the few executed without being convicted of killing anyone.

No. 66565B / Caryl Chessman
Kidnapping, 2 counts / Los Angeles
Received: July 3, 1948
Executed: May 2, 1960
Pronounced Dead: 10:12 a.m.
Weight: 160 lbs. / Height: 5' 10¼"
Age: 38 / Race: White

Chessman's criminal record began with his arrest by the L.A.P.D. on 7/15/37 on charges of suspicion of auto theft and suspicion of burglary. He was subsequently committed to the Preston School of Industry. After release, he was again arrested in 1938 and committed to Preston. On 5/17/41 he was received at San Quentin for 4 counts of Robbery 1st and 1 count of Assault with Deadly Weapon. He later escaped from the California Institution for Men on 7/16/43 and was returned to prison on 1/18/44 with an additional commitment of Robbery 1st. He was subsequently released on parole. On 7/3/48 he was received at San Quentin after having been convicted on 17 charges, two of them carrying the death penalty.

The charges were as follows: 8 counts of Robbery 1st; 2 counts of Sex perversion; 4 counts of Kidnapping, two which carried the death sentence and two carried Life Imprisonment without possibility of parole; attempted robbery; Grand Theft and Attempted Rape. Subject committed his crimes in a stolen car equipped with a spotlight covered with red cellophane. He would approach his victims who, thinking he was a patrolman, would either stop or, in the event they were already parked in an isolated spot, greet him in a friendly fashion. He was armed with a 45 cal. revolver and carried a small flash light. In the two crimes involving death penalty, he kidnapped his female victims for purpose of robbery and sexually assaulted them. One girl was recovering from a polio attack and was crippled; the second girl was later committed to a mental institution. Her condition was partially attrib-

uted to her experience with Chessman. At the time of his execution she was still in a mental hospital. At about 7:50 p.m., January 23, 1948, Chessman and a companion were arrested by two traffic investigation officers of the L.A.P.D. after an 85 mph chase. The car, finally out of control, was rammed by the officers. Defendants attempted to flee on foot. As Chessman left the car, a .45 automatic fell to the pavement. In his pocket was change wrapped in a manner similar to that stolen from a clothing store earlier in the evening and, in the car was clothing and a wallet taken in the same robbery. Subject was found guilty on 5/21/48 after a jury trial. The official court reporter was assigned to transcribe the shorthand notes of the trial and another official reporter was assigned to transcribe the shorthand notes of the trial proceedings.

Thereafter, the Supreme Court of California upheld the judgement of the lower court and Chessman began a series of appeals that lasted almost 12 years. Eight previous dates of execution were set. During his period of time on Death Row, 94 persons were executed including one woman. He wrote the book, "Cell 2455" which gained him worldwide publicity and sympathy. He smuggled out two other books, "Trial by Ordeal" and "The Face of Justice." The manuscript of a fourth book, "The Kid Was a Killer" was released to him at the request of the Los Angeles Superior Court. This book was brought out for publication about the time execution of judgement took place. While Chessman was represented by attorneys, who looked up citations for him, he did most of his own legal work.

The Executed – Who Were They?

The following are excerpts from official prison records.

No. 45041 / William Edward Hickman
Murder & Kidnap, First Degree, Los Angeles
Received: March 17, 1928
Executed: October 19, 1928
Hanged: 10:10 a.m. / Drop: 6' 0" / Dead: 10:25 a.m.
Weight: 134 lbs. / Height: 5' 4" / Age: 20 / Race: White

On December 24, 1926, Hickman arrived in Los Angeles after coming across country from Missouri in a stolen automobile. In company with Welby L. Hunt, they visited a drug store operated by C. Ivy Thoms on Huntington Drive in Los Angeles. They looked the place over and decided it was worth robbing. They returned later, armed, and attempted to rob the store. While in the store, Hickman engaged in a gun battle with a police officer at which time Thoms was shot and killed. When arrested in Pendleton, Oregon, after the commission of another murder, Hickman was armed with several weapons. He had used a 32 cal. automatic to kill Thoms. For this crime Hickman and Hunt were sentenced to life imprisonment.

On December 15, 1927, Hickman kidnapped Marion Parker, age 12 years, from the Mt. Vernon school in Los Angeles, at midday. He held her captive until the morning of the 17th at which time he took her life by choking her with a dish towel and then dismembering and mutilating her body. During the time he held her captive he made two efforts to collect $1,500 from her father as ransom. On the second attempt he met Mr. Parker at approximately 8:00 p.m. on Saturday, December 17, 1927. At the point of a sawed-off shotgun, he received $1,500 in currency and delivered to Mr. Parker the torso of Marion's body. The body was dismembered and mutilated with a large pocket knife which was offered and identified in evidence during the trial of the case.

For these two crimes, Hickman was found guilty of Murder, First Degree, and Kidnapping. He was sentenced to death and to a term of ten years to life in prison.

Dabner and Seimsen, known as "The Gas-pipe Thugs," had a record of many robberies in and about San Francisco. They were accredited to 3 other murders, each of which was accomplished by the use of a length of gas-pipe.

On October 3, 1906, Dabner and Seimsen entered the Kimmon Ginko Bank, located at 1588 O'Farrell Street, San Francisco. A few minutes before noon all employees were at lunch except M. Munekata, the manager, and A. Sasaki, a clerk. Going to a rear room of the bank, used by the manager as an office, they engaged Munekata in conversation and then bludgeoned him over the head. Calling Sasaki to the same room, they assaulted him in the same fashion. Seizing twenty-two hundred dollars in gold and silver, they left the bank. They abandoned the gas-pipe and it was found in the room with the two victims. Munekata died from the effects of a fractured skull but Sasaki recovered, appeared as a witness, and identified the two thugs.

Dabner confessed after the two were arrested a month after the killing. However, they pled not guilty to first degree murder, were tried separately, and each found guilty without recommendation. Each appealed to the State Supreme Court which affirmed the judgement and order of the Superior Court, levying the death sentence.

No. 21985 / John Seimsen
Murder, First Degree / San Francisco
Received: Jan. 26, 1907 / Executed: July 31, 1908
Hanged / Pronounced Dead / Drop 5' 7"
Weight: 168 lbs. / Height: 5' 7½" / Age 28

Hatamoto, a Japanese, had been living in illicit relationship with Ayaka Kanya, a married woman and the mother of a three year old child, Mollie Kanya, in Torrance, California. They apparently had entered into a suicide pact because of their love and the wish to stop living in their present manner. Mrs. Kanya did not care to leave the child with her father or with other relatives and they decided to kill her and then commit suicide.

Hatamoto borrowed a rifle and purchased some ammunition. They rented a house for the purpose of perpetrating the crime and the suicides. Mrs. Kanya asked that he do away with the child first.

Consequently, on December 13, 1931, Hatamoto, with the mother's knowledge and consent, took the child to a building adjacent to the house in which they were living and shot her twice. A grave was dug in a chicken yard and the body was buried. Subsequently, they lost their nerve and did not carry out their plans for suicide.

Hatamoto plead guilty of murder in the first degree and was sentenced to hang. Mrs. Kanya confessed to her part in the killing and was sentenced to life imprisonment in the Women's State Prison at Tehachapi.

No . 52794 / Koji Hatamoto
Murder, First Degree, Los Angeles
Received: September 9, 1932
Executed: May 19, 1933
Hanged: 10:01 a.m. / Dead: 10:16 a.m.
Drop: 6' 10"
Weight: 129 lbs. / Height: 5' 6$\frac{1}{8}$"
Age: 39 / Race: Japanese

No . 43921 / Earl J. Clark
Murder First Degree, Los Angeles
Received: July 28, 1927
Executed: September 23, 1927
Hanged: 10:00 a.m. / Drop: 5' 8"
Pronounced Dead: 10:13 $\frac{1}{2}$ a.m.
Weight: 187 lbs.
Height: 5' 8"
Age: 37
Race: White

Earl J. Clark is the inmate referred to by Dr. Stanley when he describes his experience at an execution. (See pages 7 and 8)

The deceased, Silva, 3 other sailors from a steamship lying in Los Angeles Harbor at San Pedro, and two taxi drivers drove to the home of Earl J. Clark, four or five miles from San Pedro, on the evening of April 18, 1925. Clark, illegally selling liquor, had with him a girl that he was keeping for immoral purposes. After a half hour an altercation took place between Clark and Silva. It began in the room occupied by the girl but soon moved to the main room of the house with the other men. The cause of the argument is not clear. A scuffle took place and Clark was seen to stab Silva two or three times in the abdomen. Immediately thereafter, all persons left the house in two vehicles. The four sailors returned to their ship. Silva did not complain of being injured and gave no indications that he had been stabbed. Each sailor returned to his room and in a few minutes Silva shouted for aid, being in great pain. He died a few hours later. Witnesses to the argument testified they saw movements during the scuffle that lead them to believe Clark had stabbed Silva. Only one was certain of seeing a knife. The next day a knife was found on the premises.

Clark plead not guilty and while waiting trial escaped from the Los Angeles County Jail. He was recaptured after several months. He was sentenced to death and the State Supreme Court affirmed the judgement of the Superior Court.

The unclaimed bodies of prisoners who died at San Quentin were buried on a hill outside the gates. Each year, on Memorial Day, members of the Salvation Army would place flowers on the graves. This picture was taken in the 1920's.

Like the warden, the locksmith is required to live on the prison property. He could be considered one of the most important people at San Quentin, at least by the inmates. On occasion, inmates will fidget with the locks on their cells. This jams them and causes the prisoner to become a "prisoner" in his own cell. The locksmith is called upon to set them "free."

A page of poetry by inmates, 1936.

JANUARY — FEBRUARY, 1936   15

THE CAGED POETS
A MISCELLANY OF INMATE POETRY

My Valentine

THERE'S a merry twinkle in the eyes
       of Valentine
As he peeps at me through little
       frills of lace.
Beckons me to leave my sorrow, 'round
My heart soft fingers twine,
And again I see the vision of a lovely,
       lonely face.
           —EMERSON SOUKUP

Give Me Words

Give me words to breathe into troubled hearts,
Jewelled words, that scale the lifting walls of
Anguish, and let them drop while each imparts
A healing potion: sympathetic love
To all in wanton torment wrought. No judge
Am I, nor would I ever be, for I
Have learned bitterly, that when I begrudge
The single word of hope, when I pass by
With no interchange of praise — then unheard
I've lost the gift more precious far than gold,
The silver phrase coined from a jewelled word.
Give back again those words I let grow cold,
To warm against my breast for future use,
To drop in tenderness, and not abuse.
           —JEAN WILSON

Novice

Farewell! The sun shall find the blade no more!
The trees shall wave upon the hills, and snow
Shall sprinkle lightly on the trembling bough . . .
But long-lost souls will fill this vale before
I return anew. Poppies sway in restless
Rhythm, seeking to be gone from here;
They long to hear the joyous laughter near
Of children at their play, delightfully helpless,
To curb the tides that wash upon the shore of life.
Embedded in child's simplicity,
Ever abounding in pure humility,
I sought and found the truth for evermore.

And so . . . farewell! The ways of civilization
Can never bring my dreams to realization!
           —BURMAH WHITE

A Stubborn Chil'

Fie! Fie upon you stubborn Ethiop man!
You fail to comprehend Il Duce's plan.
You should not thus resist beneficence
     Which seeks your weal alone in its offense.

You know that crass ineptitude should yield
To such well wishing gentry when afield,
Whose sole desire it is to civilize
     The backward and barbaric enterprise,

Which in futility you style your home.
Now come! Accept these blessings for your own.
With philanthropic zeal they send to you,
     Their planes, and poison gas, and war tanks too:

All guaranteed to yield an ordered state,
With farmsteads neat and countryside ornate,
And cities stately, all in fine repair;
     Although, Alack! YOU will not be their heir.
           —JAY WOODS

Vagabond Thoughts

MY THOUGHTS, as ragged vagabonds, roam
Down burly pathways I once have known.
Up through the air, on land, at sea;
Regardless of me, they remain free.
Recalling a snatch of song that thrills,
The touch of a hand, or a word that fills
My exiled heart with longing to be
As heedless as they are gay and carefree.
Then the droning sounds of the old hall clock
Announce it is time for the doors to lock.

Alone, the setting sun beckons to me —
Vagabond thoughts answer — for they are free.
           —VELMA WILLIAMS

Honest Abe

With life his school he fought his way
From lonely forest to the heights;
He read while plowing fields each day,
Ambition filled his cabined nights.

In after years, his work complete,
He planned to take his well-earned rest,
But Fate decreed his lone defeat.
With the immortals he is blest.
           —EMERSON SOUKUP

Northcott was convicted of the murder of an unknown Mexican boy on or about February 1, 1928. Also, the murders of Nelson and Lewis Winslow on or about May 26, 1928. Northcott, it is contended and he admitted, was a moral pervert and a degenerate of the lowest type. He was living with his mother and his nephew, Sanford Clark, on a ranch in Riverside County. He shot the Mexican boy, whose body was found nude and headless, dumped the body into a ditch near Puente, took the head to the ranch, and attempted to destroy it by burning and chopping it up with an axe. The two Winslow boys were either kidnapped or abducted while returning home after a boy's club meeting. They were held in captivity at Northcott's ranch for 10 - 12 days, forced to submit to immoral practices on the part of Northcott, and then were killed by being beaten with an axe. The bodies were buried in a chicken yard on the ranch. Sanford Clark told of Northcott's immoral practices and the murders, saying that Northcott had forced him to take a hand in the killings. When suspicion was finally directed towards Northcott, he fled to Canada, was extradited and brought back for trial. He told many conflicting stories but a great deal of evidence was uncovered, proving conclusively his guilt. At least one other disappearance and murder of a boy was blamed upon him but it could not be proven. Northcott's mother, because of her knowledge of the crimes, was convicted of Murder, First Degree, and sentenced to life imprisonment in the Women's State Prison.

No . 46597 / Gordon Stewart Northcott
Murder First Degree, 3 Counts,
Riverside County
Received: February 12, 1929
Executed: October 2, 1930
Hanged: 10:06 a.m. / Drop: 5' 10 1/2"
Pronounced Dead: 10:21 a.m.
Weight: 166 lbs.
Height: 5' 9"
Age: 22 (1930) / Race: White

No . 23954 / Willie Luis
Murder First Degree,
San Luis Obispo
Received: November 30, 1909
Executed: December 6, 1912
Hanged: 9:59 1/2 a.m. / Drop: 5' 5"
Pronounced Dead: 10:11 1/2 a.m.
Weight: 181 lbs. Height: 5' 6 3/8"
Age: 44 (1912) / Race: Chinese

Louis, or Luis, a Chinese, was convicted of the murder of his mother, Gon Yin Luis, as she lay in her bed on the morning of September 30, 1909 in San Luis Obispo. He admitted to the killing. The gun used was found in a watercloset in the home, where he admitted having hidden it. No motive for the crime is known. However, he pled not guilty to first degree murder and was tried and convicted by a jury without recommendation. He appealed to the State Supreme Court which affirmed the judgement and order of the Superior Court. Because of the legal battles he remained on San Quentin's Condemned Row over three years before being hanged.

The Early Years

Gold was the magic word! They came from everywhere. The dreamers, the adventuresome, the young and old to strike it rich! Why, there was gold all over the place – everywhere!

Sometimes, just on the rumor of a new gold find, people flocked to a site. Five, ten, twenty thousand men would journey into an area and virtually create a town overnight. Towns like Columbia, Sierra City, Hangtown, and that crown jewel of cities – San Francisco!

November 5, 1857

"Today at 2:30 p.m. some of the prisoners were shoving a sloop loaded with wood off the wharf opposite Guard Post No. 10. The guard thinking the convicts were trying to make an escape hailed them several times to leave the boat. No attention was paid to his order. The guard fired the cannon loaded with grape shot among them, killing one instantly and wounding six more."

16

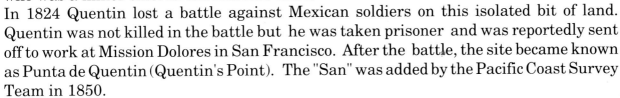

Just as life was fast and hard, so was justice. By the time California became a state in 1850, it needed a state prison. Before 1851 county jails were used in lieu of a state penitentiary pending the construction of one. On July 7, 1852, twenty acres of land was purchased, for $10,000, from Benjamin Buckalew on a site known as Point Quentin. The site was named after an Indian warrior who was a minor chief in the Licatuit tribe. In 1824 Quentin lost a battle against Mexican soldiers on this isolated bit of land. Quentin was not killed in the battle but he was taken prisoner and was reportedly sent off to work at Mission Dolores in San Francisco. After the battle, the site became known as Punta de Quentin (Quentin's Point). The "San" was added by the Pacific Coast Survey Team in 1850.

All the dreams did not come true and only a few made great fortunes. The miners, whores, and saloon keepers were a rough bunch. There were fights over mining claims and fights over the women. Stealing was an easier way to obtain gold than working all day by a streambed. They drank and they gambled. They fought and they stole. And, they killed each other.

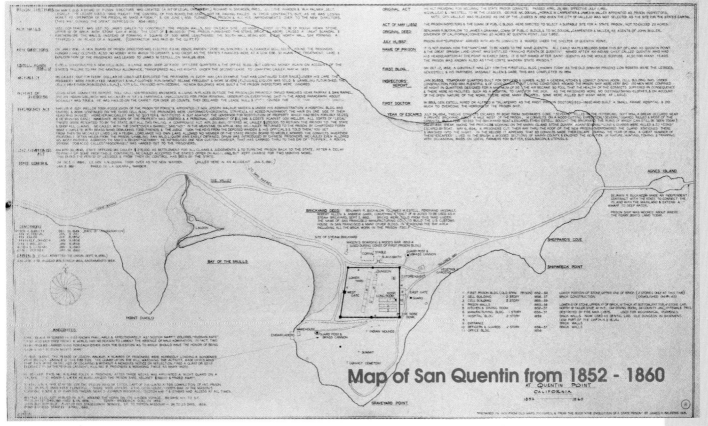

Map of San Quentin from 1852 - 1860
AT QUENTIN POINT
CALIFORNIA
1852   1860

General Mariano Vallejo, one of the first lessees for San Quentin Prison in the 1800's.

Although California had purchased the land for a prison the state had no intentions of operating it. The original concept was for the prison to be a profit making concession. It would be a leased operation with the lessees paying the state a fee for the right to operate the prison. The lessee would then hire out the prisoners to do various types of work such as making bricks, building roads, or manufacturing products. The money earned from this work would be used to pay the state its fees, provide housing, food, clothing, and guards for the prisoners plus, provide some profit for the lessee. General Mariano Vallejo and General James Estell were the first lessees for San Quentin.

On July 14, 1852, an old bark, the Waban, was towed across San Francisco Bay. It made a brief stop at Angel Island to pick up approximately 50 state prisoners and take them to Point Quentin.

Inmates "hanging out" by the Old Spanish Prison.

The Ball & Chain.

An excerpt from the Prison Log on August 27, 1857: *Lee Shell (#1088) was further punished by having one side of his head shaved and having a big chain and weight put on his leg.*

The old Dungeon, today it is used as a storeroom.

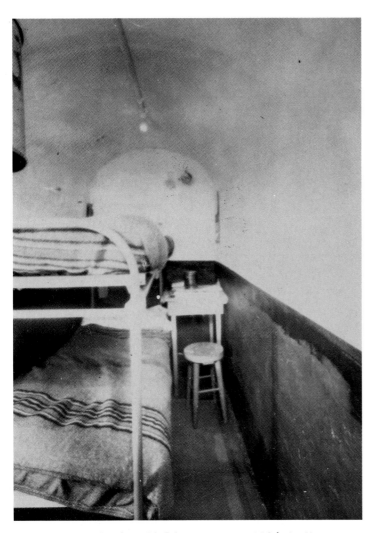

A cell in the Old Spanish Prison measured 10 1/2' x 6'.

By the end of the first year the inmate population on the ship had tripled.

While living on board the Waban, the inmates built their own prison. A site was prepared and a brick factory along with a rock quarry were established. In January of 1854 the old Spanish prison was completed. It was so called because of its Spanish colonial architecture. The building was 180' long and 24' wide. On the first floor was a dormitory and the turnkey's office. The second floor contained 48 cells. These cells were designed for 2 inmates but more often held as many as six. The cells measured 10½' x 6'. By the beginning of 1855 the building was overcrowded with more than 300 inmates. It remained in use until 1959.

In order for the prison to make a profit costs had to be kept low. Those first years were filled with much scandal. The guards were poorly paid, the food was terrible, and the living conditions were brutal. Corruption, graft, escapes, and blatant sexual activity between female prisoners with the male guards and inmates made the place a nightmare for the state. Efforts to reform the prisoners were attempted almost from the start.

In 1855, California decided the lease system was not going to work and took over the facility. There was much political bickering in Sacramento on how to run the prison. General Estell was eventually

The Old Hospital. Today, the building is used for offices.

General J. P. Ames was the first warden for San Quentin from 1880 - 1883.

A letter from Henry Myers (#21800) to Attorneys Harlan and Martin, asking them to represent him.

Quentin. An ornate Victorian mansion was constructed on the prison site as his residence. In 1880, the first official warden, J. P. Ames, was appointed.

brought back to San Quentin a little after one year of state control. Once again it was unsuccessful. In 1858, the state again took over the prison and it has continued under state control. Part of the duties for the lieutenant governor of California, at that time, was acting warden of San

The warden's residence as it appeared in 1875.

An inmate clerk recording in the daily log.

The daily log.

PRISON LOG OF THE DAY

March 1, 1856:

Information having been given that several of the men who sleep in the long rooms were in the habit of indulging in the most disgusting propensities, a strict inquiry was made, and the guilty were punished by the amount of lashes set opposite the names, by the Deputy Warden.

Antonio Joaquin (#847)	*30 lashes*
Ignancio Montera (#544)	*15 lashes*
Lorenzo Nieblas (#741)	*12 lashes*
Visalia Padilles (#671)	*12 lashes*

Whole number of prisoners: 420

July 11, 1872:

Still continuing to blow terribly, and is quite cool and sharp, wind from the North West. One prisoner taken out by order of Court on another charge. Sanitary measures adopted by Resident Director Lieutenant Governor Pacheco for the prevention of the spread of small pox. A case having been reported on the point. All persons are thereby forbidden to enter the yard from the infected premises and no more visitors allowed inside until further notice.

Whole number of prisoners, 924.

July 4, 1874:

Cool and a little cloudy, no work done in the shops on this day. Ten guns fired this morning sunrise breaking the glass badly at the posts and jarring all the buildings inside the walls. Prisoners in Room 3 held a ball last night and enjoyed themselves hugely. All is quiet in prison and this makes it three 4ths of July that I have been imprisoned, two in San Quentin and one in Tulare County jail. K. H. Keeny.

Whole number of prisoners, 973.

November 16, 1874:

Morning cloudy, wind in the North West. One prisoner escaped today by drilling through the door in No. 4 Cell. Stone Building, secured ladders in the cabinet shop and scaled the walls at the Tannery.

Whole number of prisoners, 1013.

Ladies Of The House

"Ladies of the House," in costume to perform at a New Year's Eve show in the 1920's.

From 1856 to 1933, over 81 years, women were held as inmates at San Quentin. This may come as a surprise for many since there is little documentation at San Quentin about female prisoners. The stories which have been told are usually related in some form of a salacious episode. Female inmates were often portrayed as sex-starved Amazons. The stories about trap doors in women's cells, to let in men, would have been improbable at San Quentin. It was unlikely that the women committed to state prison, during the late 1800's and early 1900's, were "nice ladies." It was also highly unlikely that they were all of the same mold. Just who were Agnes Read, Dolores Martinez, Nellie Mague, May Von and the other women at San Quentin?

While little research has been done on the female inmates a few personalities have been documented. The following women represent a few of the "ladies" at San Quentin. A young native American girl known only as Isobel (#993) was the youngest female to be sent to San Quentin. She was convicted of manslaughter, in 1856, when only 13 years old. Her

The courtyard inside the building where the captain's office was located. Female inmates were housed above the captain's office until 1885.

companion in crime was a man named Rafael. Records show they were convicted in Contra Costa County. However, the records do not show what became of her.

While the annals of western folklore talk of male train robbers, no mention is made of Modesta Avila (#13793). After attempting to wreck a train, she was traced to her San Francisco Barbary Coast hideout and arrested. There had been several reports at the time that trains had been wrecked and robbed by a woman. Avila was convicted only of the attempt and received a 3 year sentence to San Quentin in 1889.

Francesca de la Guerra (#19967) served the shortest sentence – 1 day. The 42 year old San Franciscan saleslady was convicted of bigamy. She arrived on February 4, 1903 and was released on February 5, 1903.

Emma McVicar Le Doux (#24077) was the infamous "Trunk Murderer". The press of 1906 had a field day with this story and Le Doux dominated the headlines for months. She had given her husband Albert McVicar knockout drops, hit him on the head, then put his body in a trunk. On March 24, 1906, an awful odor as well as leaks were coming from a trunk left at the Stockton, California, Southern Pacific Depot. Authorities opened the trunk and inside was McVicar's body. Shortly thereafter, Le Doux was arrested. She was convicted of first degree murder and was the first woman sentenced to hang in California.

During the appeal process, a compromise was reached and her sentence was reduced to life imprisonment. Le Doux was paroled a few times but she always ended back in prison. She died on July 7, 1941, at age 69, in state prison.

Emma McVicar Le Doux, #24077, the famous "Trunk Murderer."

Life at San Quentin was extremely bleak for the women. While some attempt was made to provide entertainment for them, the meager forms of amusement chosen only emphasized their limited and cloistered environment. In 1916 the women were able to listen to a "concert" – on a phonograph. Movies were occassionally shown and on Christmas day, in 1922, there was a "fashion parade."

The women were housed above the captain's office until 1885. Later the building was enlarged to provide them with a separate wing. Their main occupation was sewing prison uniforms. There was never a large number of women at San Quentin. In 1907, there were 27 and the total seldom went higher than 50 at any one time.

A typical woman's cell in Bayview.

California's Institution for Women at Tehachapi, 1936.

In 1924, the state of California decided that the women should have their own building. It was constructed outside the prison walls on the site known as South Point. The new building contained individual cells with windows and some storage space. Completed in 1927 it was nicknamed "Bayview." Women occupied this facility until 1933. They were moved when the new institution at Tehachapi was built. This new prison was operated as an off-site department of San Quentin until 1937. Thereafter, the California Institution of Women became a separate facility.

Bayview, the women's wing, was completed in 1927.

The early prison log was limited with information about the women inmates. The following briefly describes their lives "inside the walls."

October 22, 1872:
This has been quite a pleasant day, but we had quite a lively shock of an earthquake this afternoon. One prisoner arrived from Sacramento today.

Rev. Mathews and Sister Mary Barry visited the office this afternoon. Sister Barry was on a visit to her sister who is an inmate in the female department.
Whole number of prisoners, 914.

February 3, 1873:
Weather mild and pleasant and the wind is coming from the north. Service was held in the chapel today. This afternoon the wind changed from north to south and coming in very strong. It looks as though it would blow up a storm. The women's department went on a rampage this afternoon and there were fisticuffs exchanged between two women and the matrons.
Whole number of prisoners, 903.

October 24, 1873:
Clear, cold morning, feels like frost with little wind blowing from the North West. Three prisoners discharged today by expiration of sentence.

Mary Dugan's little girl was taken from the prison today.
Whole number of prisoners, 924.

Who was the sister of Sister Mary Barry, what was her name and why was she doing time? What started the "rampage" which occurred on February 3, 1873? And, Mary Dugan's little girl, was the child born to her while she was an inmate?

While the last resident left "Bayview" in 1933, women today are still not free of San Quentin. Since the prison is the only place designated to perform executions in California, women are returned here to be put to death. All four women executed in California were brought to San Quentin several days before and confined in the hospital until the day of their execution.

The four women executed – what were their crimes? Three of the four were over 50 years old. Only one carried out her crime alone. While most of the executed men had killed wives or girlfriends, none of these women were executed for killing a husband or lover.

Eithel Leta Juanita Spinelli, known as "The Duchess," was executed on November 21, 1941. She was the first woman to be executed in California. Gordon Hawkins and Mike Simone, her partners in the murder of Robert Sherrard, a 19 year old member of her gang, were executed one week later on November 28, 1941. Albert Ives, who also participated in the murder, turned state's evidence. He was later judged insane and committed to Mendocino State Hospital for life.

Sherrard was boasting about having killed the owner of a San Francisco barbecue stand. Spinelli was afraid she would be exposed and ordered Sherrard's death. She gave him knockout drops in a drink. When he was unconscious, her three partners dumped him into the Sacramento River.

Warden Clinton Duffy described her as, "the coldest, hardest character, male or female, I have ever known . . . Even though I had seen pictures of the Duchess, and knew she was no beauty, I was amazed at her utter lack of feminine appeal. At fifty-two she was a homely, scrawny, nearsighted, sharp-featured scarecrow, with thin lips, beady eyes, and scraggly black hair flecked with gray. It hardly seemed possible that even young punks, with neither brains nor character, would take orders from her."

The second was Louise Peete, executed on April 11, 1947. Peete was first convicted for murder in 1921 and paroled in 1939. A parole that Warden Duffy deemed, "a horrible mistake."

She was described as, "a wholesome looking, stylish, handsomely plump matron with a peaches-and-cream complexion and an air of innocent sweetness which masked a heart of ice." However, an amazing number of people around her seemed to die. She was married three times but all of her husbands mysteriously "committed suicide." A hotel clerk, who befriended her, killed himself, and a woman roommate became very ill and died suddenly.

In 1944, she was convicted and sentenced to die for the shooting of Margaret Logan. After killing Mrs. Logan, Peete moved into the Logan home, had Mr. Logan committed to a mental hospital, then began disposing of their property. It was not until several months later that she was apprehended, while still living in the Logan home.

No . 66728
Eithel Leta Juanita Spinelli
Murder, First Degree
Sacramento County
Received: Nov. 20, 1941
Executed: Nov. 21, 1941
Hanged: 10:14 a.m.
(Cyanide Dropped)
Dead: 10:25 a.m.
Weight: 134 lbs. / Height: 5' 5"
Age: 50 / Race: White

No . 35692A
Louise Peete
Murder, First Degree
Los Angeles via Tehachapi
Received: April 10, 1947
Executed: April 11, 1947
Lethal Gas
Dead: 10:13 a.m.
Weight: 157½ lbs.
Height: 5' 3"
Age: 58 / Race: White

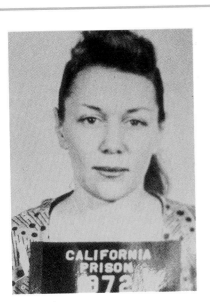

No . CIW 1972
Barbara Graham
Murder, First Degree
Los Angeles
Received: October 14, 1953
Executed: June 3, 1955
Dead: 11:42 a.m.
Weight: 121 lbs. / Height: 5' 4"
Age: 32 / Race: White

No . CIW 3249
Elizabeth Ann Duncan
Murder, First Degree
Subornation of Perjury & Forgery
Ventura
Received: April 3, 1959
Executed: August 8, 1962
Dead: 10:12 a.m.
Weight: 165 lbs. / Height: 5' 4"
Age: 58 / Race: White

Barbara Graham, who was depicted in the movie "I Want To Live" starring Susan Hayward, is perhaps the best known of the four. A retired correctional officer disagrees with the movie's sympathetic portrayal of Ms. Graham. His recollection of her was, "an incredibly foul-mouthed tramp."

Graham, along with John Santo, Emmett Perkins, Baxter Shorter, and John True broke into the home of Mabel Monohan, intending to rob her of $100,000. Monohan was beaten beyond recognition and died as a result of a brain hemorrhage. Graham, Santo and Perkins were convicted and executed. True testified for the state and was dismissed. Shorter was kidnapped before his trial and is presumed dead.

The last woman executed was Elizabeth Ann "Ma" Duncan on August 8, 1962. According to prison records, Mrs. Duncan was extremely upset that her son, Frank, had married a nurse named Olga against her wishes. Records state that Mrs. Duncan first tried to have the marriage annulled. She hired a man named Ralph Winterstein to act as her son and appear in court testifying he wanted an annulment. This did not work and Mrs. Duncan was later convicted of trying to fraudulently obtain an annulment.

According to state records, Mrs. Duncan then hired Augustine Baldonado and Luis Moya to kill Olga for $6,000. In November, 1958, the evil act was carried out. All three were convicted of Olga's murder and all three died in San Quentin's gas chamber.

In spite of stereotypical stories about female prisoners, women at San Quentin were tightly sequestered. What was prison like for them? Were there no diaries, letters or journals ever written? What happened to the small number of children born to these women, while they were inmates? Are any of the women imprisoned at San Quentin during the 20's and 30's alive today? What stories could be told . . .

Women have returned to San Quentin but this time as Correctional Officers. Associate Warden R. A. Nelson says, "As a 32 year veteran of the system, I was very skeptical as to whether women could handle the job of working with male inmates. My concerns have been proven groundless. On the whole, they are excellent officers. In some instances, such as ones in which an inmate may need to prove how tough he is to another man, a female officer can actually better diffuse aggression."

The Famous
And The Infamous

C. E. Bolton, alias Black Bart.

Black Bart

I rob the rich to pay the poor,
which hardly is a sin,

A widow ne'er knocked at my door,
but what I let her in.

So don't blame me for what I've done,
I don't deserve your curses,

And if for any cause I'm hung,
let it be for my verses.

Black Bart

C. E. Bolton, alias Black Bart, was probably the most notorious of the legendary stagecoach bandits of the old west.

Between 1875 and 1883, Black Bart robbed 28 Wells Fargo stages. His robberies were nearly identical. He wore a flour sack with eye holes over his head, carried a double barreled shotgun, and "Throw down that box!" was his trademark command. What made him a romantic legend of boldness and determination were the poems he left at the scene of the crime. To the stagecoach passengers he was chivalrous - he never robbed any of them. To the law he was a phantom.

He was wounded on his 28th robbery but escaped. True to legend the fatal clue left behind was a handkerchief. Through the laundry mark it was traced to San Francisco and C. E. Bolton was arrested on November 12, 1883. Tried in San Andreas, he pled guilty and was sentenced to San Quentin and became inmate #11046 until his discharge on January 21, 1888.

Black Bart was never heard from again. But the legend did not die. There were rumors of him going to the China coast and of his being in Mexico. And, while Wells Fargo always denied it, rumors persisted that they were paying Black Bart a large salary not to rob their stage coaches. But, by then, the 54 year old former school teacher and Civil War hero, who neither smoked or drank and who wrote poetry for a pastime, had already made his place as a folk hero of the old west.

Free Tom Mooney

Photograph used in a 1936 campaign by organized labor to get Tom Mooney released from prison.

"Free Tom Mooney!" was a popular labor union battle cry. A bomb exploded during the 1916 San Francisco Preparedness Parade killing 16 people. Mooney, a member of the International Molder's Union, was convicted and received a life sentence for his part in the bombing. He immediately became a symbol of organized labor persecution.

Clint Duffy claimed Mooney was the most irritating of the prima donna inmates who was always acting the role of a martyr to the hilt. Says Duffy, "I've always thought that Mooney would have been happier if he had spent his life in prison where he had a certain status that he never could have enjoyed outside. This was substantiated after Governor Olson pardoned him in 1939. A fairly sizable crowd welcomed Tom at the front gate but soon thereafter, his popularity swiftly melted. He was a forgotten man within a few months and "Free Tom Mooney!," now a fait accompli, became a forgotten slogan. Mooney died in obscurity not long after he left San Quentin."

Strange but True . . .

Robert Wells, while an inmate at San Quentin in 1938, helped to build the gas chamber in which he would be executed in 1942. Wells was a small man, 4'10", and he was very good with precise mechanical assembly. He was just the right man to connect the complex rods, pipes, tubes and set the gauges for the gas chamber.

In 1941, shortly after completing the chamber, Wells was paroled. He then killed his brother, sister-in-law and her friend. They had put an end to a love affair Wells was having with his half-sister. He was returned to San Quentin after his conviction to be executed.

Robert Wells

29

The Mind Of A Multiple Murderer

James P. Watson, "Bluebeard."

James P. Watson, known as "Bluebeard," killed at least 15 wives, possibly 22, maybe more. He arrived at San Quentin in May of 1920 and died there in 1939. Watson avoided the gallows by giving the location of the body of Nina Deloney. In return he was given immunity from the death sentence. Nina was one of the few women he did not marry before killing.

Clinton Duffy said of Watson, "Indescribably homely . . . he was a scrawny little man who certainly didn't look the part of a lethal Don Juan . . . a fussy, guerulous griper who drove Warden Holohan mad with picayune complaints."

While serving his time at San Quentin Watson worked in the prison hospital. Dr. Leo Stanley, chief physician at the time, described Watson as, "a short, skinny, stooped wisp of fifty . . . he had the eyes of a sick rat."

So why did all of these women find this man attractive enough to marry? The following are Watson's own words. They are excerpts from conversations recorded in the journal of Dr. Stanley.

I would drive to a new city and put an ad in a paper, usually along these lines: 'Gentleman, neat appearance, courteous disposition, well connected in business, has bank account and government bonds, would be pleased to correspond with refined young lady or widow, object matrimony. This advertisement is in good faith and all answers will be treated with every respect.'

These ads led me to all types of women. I had no particular preference. I would correspond with them, and send them flowers, and visit them. I must admit, in all modesty, that my attentions were never repulsed. Of course, I couldn't possibly marry them all, but I kept up a steady exchange of letters. I never forgot a birthday or holiday.

My technique with women was simple. First, I studied the character of every woman I met, her personality, strong points, weaknesses, prejudices, and particularly what were her preconceived ideas of what a man should be. Then I molded myself into that dream man.

I have told the most improbable and impossible tales to women and seen them accepted without a sign of suspicion.

If I suspected that a woman is of a home loving type, I would hold up visions of a home with luxurious furnishings, of a position as a banker's wife in a small western town. This dream life was to take place a few months after the wedding when I would retire. Until then I would say they were bound to secrecy about our engagement because I was a government detective engaged in important secret work. This way, I escaped police detection and also accounted for long absences.

If she seemed fond of going out, I spoke of a trip around the world, of jewels and beautiful clothes, of a life of ease.

No matter what type she was I covered her in a blanket of solicitude and devotion. Few men ever give the feeling of protection and well being I conveyed with my attentions. These little signs of consideration are never overlooked by a woman. If she dropped anything, I picked it up before she realized she had dropped it, I helped her with her coat, stood up when she did, noticed a different hair style or a new dress.

I never failed to let a woman know that I was proud of her, that every man was envious of me, and had a right to be. Whenever I took her out, I was as one oblivious to my surroundings, spellbound by this fascinating creature. I made her feel that I had never seen anyone quite like her and that at last, I had found the one woman meant for me, the one woman I had spent a lifetime waiting for.

I courted several women at all times. The ones I picked for my wives I picked on a whim. The first four or five women I chose because of the red coloring. It was as though they were teasing me, hiding that delicious blood, letting it peek ever so slightly through the cheeks. Then I killed a dried-up type. It was a surprise, you know, like opening up a dry old pomegranate and finding all those juicy little things inside.

I spent all my time daydreaming about my women. The one I most frequently dreamed of killing was usually the one I married.

The trouble with the murders was that they never quite worked out the way I wanted them to. They struggled and squirmed too much. As they died, I had an ejection and a wonderful feeling of power, of release. It was a sort of an ecstasy that no words could describe.

Sometimes I strangled them to bring out that incomparable dark red hue to their faces. Then, of course, I missed wiping up the blood.

I loved wiping up the blood after the murder. It made me feel as though I were drinking it in, as though I were assimilating the person and thereby gaining new strength. There was something to vampire stories, I think. I'm sorry that I only caught on to a good trick with Nina [Deloney]. I strangled her first then beat her over the head with a hammer.

Then I would undress them completely. Nothing gives a man such a feeling of omnipotence as viewing the naked body of a woman he has just bludgeoned to death.

Nina was one of my best. Do you know what I discovered when I undressed her? She had a secrect pocket sewed in her camisole and in it she had a fortune in jewels I'd never heard about. In addition, there were seven one thousand dollar bonds and two five hundred dollar bonds.

After a slaying, I would get a good nap. When I woke up, I'd have resumed my interest in all my women. I'd have a good meal and start thinking up new compliments for my girls."

Held Hostage

On April 21, 1959, William Werner and Billy Joe Wright escaped from a prison work detail.

The two men held Louise Gschwend hostage at knife point on a fishing pier. Douglas Harrison was forced to act as intermediary between them and prison officials. Werner and Wright surrendered without incident six hours later.

Wright was later transferred to Folsom State Prison and Werner was sent to the California Medical Facility at Vacaville for psychiatric treatment.

William Werner being led from the pier after his surrender. To his left is officer Al Mello, one of the founders of the Correctional Officer's Union – the C.C.P.O.A.

Mrs. Louise Gschwend, middle aged San Francisco housewife, talks to reporters right after she was released by Billy Joe Wright and William Werner.

William D. Werner, 24, left, prior to being transferred to adjustment section of Folsom State Prison. Billy Joe Wright, 26, right, was sent to the California Medical Facility at Vacaville for psychiatric treatment.

August 21, 1971

This represents excerpts from the San Francisco Examiner, Sunday, August 22 and Monday, August 23, 1971 issues.

San Francisco Examiner
MONARCH OF THE DAILIES

| Vol. 1971, No. 34 | ☆☆☆☆☆ | SUNDAY, AUGUST 22, 1971 | SU 1-2424 |

Get-Tough Rule Near In Prisons

A new get-tough policy aimed at controlling the state prison system's "revolutionaries" and "worst incorrigibles" may be in the offing as a result of Saturday's San Quentin bloodletting.

"We are moving in the direction of having closer custody of many of the people we suspect of revolutionary type activities." State Corrections Director Raymond K. Procunier said at San Quentin yesterday.

3 Guards, 3 Cons Slain In Quentin Break Try

'Jackson Hid Gun in Hair'

"His plan had been blown." Park said of Jackson's desperate actions, "it was his only options."

When Jackson and DeLeon got back to the adjustment center where a skin search was started, another guard noticed the gun. "The officer saw something up there (in Jackson's head) but probably didn't know at that point it was a gun," the warden said.

KILLED IN SAN QUENTIN DESPERATE JAILBREAK TRY
Guards Paul Krasenes, Frank DeLeon, and Jere Graham

Life at San Quentin is not easy and some days can be nightmare. Hundreds of articles analyzing the events of August 21, 1971 have been printed. The following is an account from one man who was there. These are his words written immediately after the events occurred.

TO: A. R. Jacobs, Associate Warden, Custody

SUBJECT: Major Incident in the Adjustment Center on 8/21/71.

At approximately 2:55 p.m. this date, I received a telephone call at my home on the Institution grounds from the Institution telephone operator informing me that Inmate Jackson, A-63837, and another inmate had just escaped from the Adjustment Center, and were running through the yard, and Jackson had what looked to be a gun in his possession.

I immediately left for the Institution, arriving there at approximately 3:00 p.m. As I entered the between-gates area I was met by Lts. Luxford and Stewart, who informed me that Jackson had been shot, and was lying in the road way just beyond the Chapel complex. I proceeded to the area where I saw Jackson lying on his back on the ground. He appeared to be dead from a bullet wound in the area of the head.

Inmate Spain, B8672, the other inmate who escaped with Jackson, was also lying on the ground a few yards from Jackson. He was alive and appeared to be uninjured. I later learned that Spain had hid in the bushes when the shots were fired and was eventually removed from there, and placed on the road way.

Lt. Luxford informed me that they did not know what was taking place in the Adjustment Center. They were unable to contact any personnel by telephone and no one could be visibly seen in the officer area when they looked through the windows. I ordered Lt. Luxford to secure weapons from the armory in order to arm a task force to enter the Adjustment Center building. These weapons were to consist of shotguns, rifles, and Thompson sub-machine guns.

33

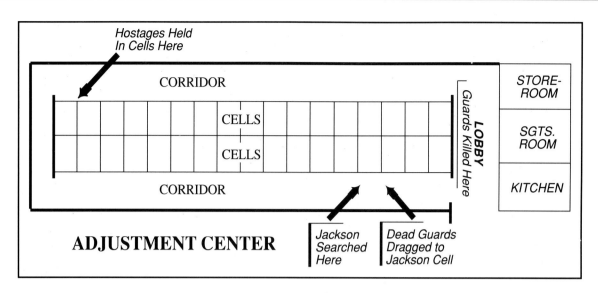

Hostages Held In Cells Here

CORRIDOR

CELLS

CELLS

CORRIDOR

LOBBY Guards Killed Here

STORE-ROOM

SGTS. ROOM

KITCHEN

ADJUSTMENT CENTER

Jackson Searched Here

Dead Guards Dragged to Jackson Cell

At approximately 3:20 p.m., weapons were secured from the armory and issued to eight custodial personnel. I then ordered the door to the Adjustment Center to be opened and we proceeded with weapons in ready position to enter the Adjustment Center. When we entered the building, we encountered no one; however, we noted that the locking device door was open, and the security door leading into the north side cell area was open. We called down the way and received no response. As far as I could see, all cell doors were open and an inmate could be seen on the floor with the upper part of his body lying out on the tier. He seemed to be severly cut in the area of the neck. I dispatched four of the armed officers to the south side to stand guard while the other four of us started in to the north side, and slowly checked each cell as we went. When we arrived at cell 1 AC 3, where the inmate was lying on the floor, we found four Correctional personnel. Three were piled on the bed and the fourth was lying on the floor of the cell. All four appeared to be in serious condition or dead. The cell was covered with blood. Two officers looked like they had been strangled and all appeared to have been cut in the area of the neck. An officer was dispatched to get gurneys and help. Within minutes other staff with hospital attendants arrived. All officers and the inmate were placed on gurneys and transported to the prison hospital. I was later informed that three of the officers, Officer De Leon, Krasenes, and Sgt. Graham had been pronounced dead at the prison hospital. The fourth man, Sgt. McCray was seriously injured. The inmate identified as Lynn, A-81702, also had been pronounced dead.

While the injured were being removed from the cell, armed officers continued to search the north side of the Adjustment Center. Two inmates were found to be barricaded in their own cells. They were identified as Inmate Hetland, B-26828, in Cell 1 AC 13, and Inmate Fisher, A-79753, in Cell 1 AC 17. These men were uninjured and were left temporarily in their cells.

After completing the search of this side, we returned to the officers' area, and went to the South side grill gate where our other officers were standing guard. It was noted on this side also, that all cell doors were open. I was informed by the officers, who had been observing, that they had seen inmate movement in the back of the south side in the area of the quiet cells. I called down on at least two occasions for the inmates to come out. At first I received no response, but later heard someone shout back, "We have hostages." I informed them that the hostages would do them no good, and instructed them to release the hostages, and allow them to come up front where we were. I then told them to come out one at a time guaranteeing them that no one would be harmed. I received no response to this request. I waited approximately one minute, and then ordered Lt. Nelson to shoot a blast of rounds from the sub-machine gun into the wall at the end of the corridor beyond where the inmates were. Approximately fifteen seconds after this was done two men came running very fast from the quiet cell area. They were clothed only in white shorts and tee shirts and were bleeding profusely from the neck and face. They were identified almost immediately as Officers Breckenridge and Rubiaco. Both men were immediately placed on gurneys and taken to the Institution hospital for medical care. Again, a call was made to the inmates to come out one at a time, to no avail. Another blast from the Thompson sub-machine gun was ordered and after a wait of approximately one minute, one inmate stepped out from the quiet cell with his hands up. He

was instructed to walk slowly towards us. When he was approximately forty feet from us, he was to stop, and remove all of his clothing. After this was accomplished, he was instructed to back up to the gate where we were standing. Once he was in our custody he was escorted out of the Adjustment Center and placed on the lawn, where handcuffs and leg irons were put on him. He was told to lay in a prone position. This procedure was followed until all inmates had been removed from the Adjustment Center. This was accomplished with only an amount of force as was necessary. All inmates were out of the Adjustment Center and the move was completed by approximately 5:30 p.m. Inmate Mancino, A92050, disobeyed the officers' orders and started to get up from the lawn where he was ordered to lay. An armed officer fired a warning shot that ricocheted and fragments hit him in the upper part of the back of the leg.

When we felt certain that all inmates had been removed, armed officers made a cell to cell search of the south side of the Adjustment Center. Upon arriving at cell 1 AC 62, an inmate was found lying prone on the bed. He appeared to be cut in the area of the throat. Another gurney was sent for and he was removed to the hospital. The inmate was later identified as Kane, B-4273, who was pronounced dead at the hospital.

A search of the garden area adjacent to the chapel was conducted as there was reason to believe that inmate Spain possibly had a gun also. The search proved negative with the exception of a set of jail keys assigned to an Adjustment Center Officer were found in the vicinity where Spain hid in the bushes.

Supervisors in the yard and cell blocks informed me that they had difficulty in getting inmates to lock-up for the count, and many threats were made against staff. It was decided at this time that no one would be fed in the mess hall, and that all inmates would receive sack lunches delivered to their cells.

Mr. Bruce Bales, District Attorney, and one of his deputies arrived to make an investigation. Director Procunier arrived at the Institution. All available information was given to him. He assigned Mr. Snellgrove and Mr. Coyle, both special investigators for the department, to assist in the investigation of the incident. Deputy Marin County Coroner, Mr. Fontaine, arrived; also, an investigating team from C. I. I., and a member of the Attorney General's staff. These investigators worked throughout the night in the Adjustment Center. At approximately 7:00 p.m. each inmate involved in the incident was read his rights, then was questioned by custodial staff. Blood samples were taken from each inmate by hospital staff.

Shortly after the escape attempt by Jackson, Plan A of our escape plan was put into effect. Units from the local law enforcement agencies patrolled the outer perimeter of the Institution. Armed sheriff's deputies and highway patrol officers were brought into the security area for back-up support and fire power.

The Institution count cleared at 7:35 p.m. and, at that time, all outside agencies were relieved of duty. At approximately 9:30 p.m., fourteen inmates housed on the south side of the second tier of the Adjustment Center were moved to B section segregation in order to accommodate the inmates from the first floor of the Adjustment Center who were still out on the lawn. When the cells were ready, the inmates on the lawn were moved two at a time to the cells just vacated. They were issued clothing, sheets, and blankets, given haircuts, and were secured for the night. Each inmate was checked by an M. T. A. This was accomplished at approximately 11:00 p.m. Extra armed officers were placed on the gun rails in the East and South Blocks. The Institution remained quiet. I departed for home at approximately 2:00 a.m.

D. R. Weber, Correctional Captain

Years of Growth
1900 to 1935

Mess Hall; 1935.

The period of greatest growth and change for San Quentin occurred during the years 1900 to 1935. Between 1907 and 1934 the inmate population rose from 1,549 to 6,397. It was also during this time that many of the more progressive concepts dealing with prison management were initiated.

Construction was started on South Block when John E. Hoyle became Warden in 1907. It was the largest cell house in the world housing 2,000 inmates. Completed in 1910, it was the first of three new buildings to house inmates. West Block was finished in 1927 and East Block in 1930. A new kitchen as well as a new mess hall were also built during Hoyle's tenure.

Warden Hoyle's philosophy was that inmates should be kept occupied with work as much like the environment outside the prison as possible. In 1906 a school was started for the inmates. They were required to attend until they could pass an 8th grade equivalency test. The concept of parole was adopted into law in the 1890's. During

Hoyle's administration its use was greatly expanded. In 1913, the striped uniform was abandoned. It was felt that they were demeaning to the inmates. The blue pant and shirt outfit, still worn by inmates today, was instituted.

In 1913, James A. Johnston became warden. He believed, "Physical examinations, medical treatments, bodily repairs, educational opportunities, spiritual guidance and [psychology] are necessary, but the habit of work is what men most need. If I had to manage a prison upon condition that I make my choice of one thing, and only one, as an agency for reform, I should unhesitatingly choose work. Just plain, honest-to-goodness work."

It was Warden Johnston who established the road camps and allowed minimum security prisoners to work. Inmates did the blasting and rough grading for a number of highways in California.

Three inmates in stripes building a snowman, 1912.

First Prison Camp at Legetts Valley, 1917.

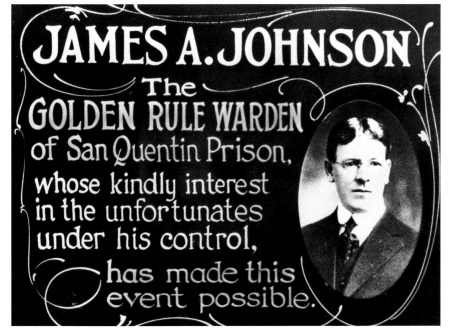

An article from a Ft. Bragg newspaper of August 25, 1915 read, "Convicts to start soon on highway. Engineer F. G. Somner has completed all arrangements to begin work on the 30 mile stretch of State Highway between Cummings and the Humboldt County line, next week. The prisoners will all be honor men and will get a material reduction on their term of sentence. They will not receive wages."

37

"Convicts to Start Soon on Highway . . .

Putting in the rough grade
for a new highway.

"All of the camp supplies are now on their way to Mendocino county. The supplies will be taken to Union Landing at the mouth of Howard Creek by boat, and then hauled about 25 miles to Legett Valley. The prisoners will come from San Quentin. This 30 miles of highway will be located in an area that now has no roads of any decription and will help settle that section."

A note from Dr. Leo Stanley's journal of 1932 describes the road camps, "The prisoners have recently completed the highway between Clear Lake and Williams in the Sacramento Valley . . . Our prison camp is in a valley about 7 miles from Wilbur Springs. The Camp

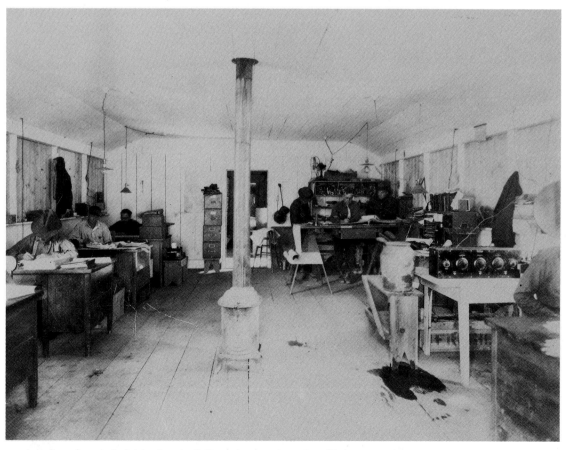

Interior of an administration building at a road camp. Note
the blueprints on the shelf and the 2-way radio on the desk.

Interior of a tent bunk house.

is located on the side of a stream amid a grove of oak trees. The bunk houses are made of wood and are heated by large stoves which burn wood fuel."

During the Great Depression free men who lacked any other way of earning a living would volunteer to work in the prison road camps. More from Dr. Stanley's journal, "The Camp . . . employed about 300 men at hand labor. These men received no wages, but had their transportation, food and some clothing furnished for them. It helped them to spend the winter which would otherwise necessitate their receiving alms at some other place. The bunk-houses are two stories in height and are lined on the inside. They are very comfortable and serviceable."

"A high number of escapes were expected from the road camps; however, they were extremely rare."

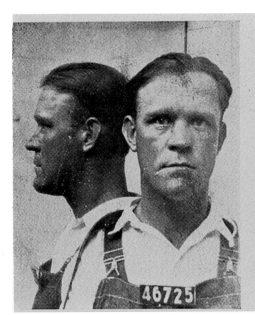

Card No. 1033   September 30 1933
STATE PRISON AT SAN QUENTIN, CAL.

ESCAPED FROM ROAD CAMP

No. 24, Oroville, Butte Co., Calif.

$200.00 Reward for Capture and Return

Name: Walter Swartz	No. 46725
Sentence: 14 & 15 Yrs. cc	County: Fresno
Crime: Asslt. to Murd. & Rob. 1st cc	Date of Arrival: 3-6-1929
Nativity: Texas	Age: 29, (1929)
Occ. Rancher Hgt.: 6 ft. 0⅞ in.	Weight: 192
Complexion: Fair Eyes: Blue	Hair: lt. Brn.

Marks and Scars: R. eye injured. Blo. scar R. brow.
            Long line scar L. side of head

FINGER PRINT CLASS: 30 IO
                       32 M

ARREST and WIRE
JAMES B. HOLOHAN, Warden, San Quentin, Cal.

39

"Inmates should be kept occupied with work in an atmosphere much like the outside."
Warden Hoyle

A school class, 1900.

During WW I flags were made in the Prison Flag Shop.

The Quarry.

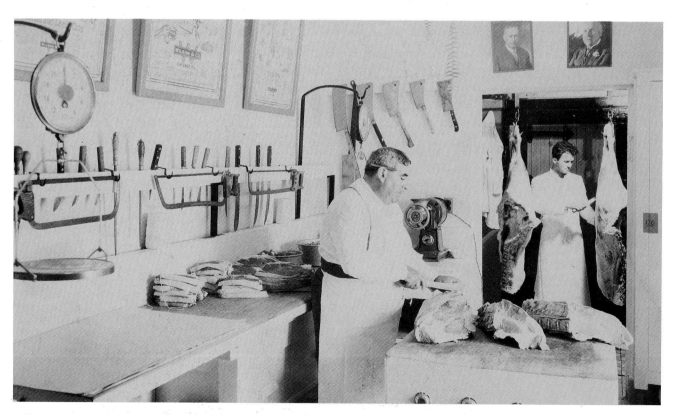

The prison butcher shop which was the forerunner of the vocation meat cutting school, 1930's.
Above the door are two portraits, left: Governor Rolph and right: Warden Holohan.

Live Performances at San Quentin.

Mme. Sarah Bernhardt performs "Une Nuit de Noel" at San Quentin in 1913. She was 69 years old at the time. Nine prisoners had small parts in the play.

There were a number of live performances, by popular entertainers, at San Quentin. Even Sarah Bernhardt performed there on February 22, 1913. Her troupe, along with 9 inmates as actors, performed a one act play, "Une Nuit de Noel Sous la Terreur," which was written by her son, Maurice Bernhardt. Popular movies as well as films of boxing matches and other sports events were shown. Douglas Fairbanks and Mary Pickford, "America's Sweetheart" also entertained at San Quentin.

Program from "Une Nuit de Noel," performed by Mme. Sarah Bernhardt.

Above: The Empress Theatre Company which came to perform at San Quentin in 1916. Below left to right: Warden James A. Johnston, Douglas Fairbanks, Sr., Mary Pickford and Pieterzak.

41

Field Day at San Quentin.

The Olympic Club Field Day at San Quentin. All of the inmates, including the dance team, are men.

The Olympic Club Field Day Bathing Beauty contest.

Aerial of the Track & Field Meet with Mt. Tamalpais in the background.

Prisoners dressed up as ladies with costumes representing different countries.

A costumed inmate "couple" at the Olympic Club sponsored annual event, 1933.

One of the more unusual diversions was the annual field day sponsored by the Olympic Club of San Francisco. The first of these was held in 1914 and as the years passed they grew in flamboyance. There were the usual track and field events. Also, there were "bathing beauty" and dance contests with inmates in costume. A parade, clowns, acrobats, tug-of-war, and a holiday meal would complete the day.

In 1924, James A. Johnston retired but later resumed his career as warden of Alcatraz Federal Penitentiary.

During James B. Holohan's tenure, 1927 to 1936, San Quentin's walls were extended, the armory tower with its drawbridge was built, as were new guard towers, a fire department, a new visitor's room and laundry facility.

The Fire Department Building. The warden's residence is located above, to the right, on the hill.

Guard post on a San Quentin prison wall.

Until 1935, Holohan could look back on a relatively tranquil 7 years as warden — there were no scandals, no major incidents or riots. Then on January 16, 1935 all hell broke loose . . .

No. 50321
Joe Kristy

On that day Holohan was dining with the parole board at the warden's residence. Four armed convicts rushed into the room and ordered the men to put up their hands. One of the prisoners put a gun to the chest of a board member and pulled the trigger. The gun misfired and the board member was unharmed. When Holohan tried to call for help, one of the convicts, Rudolph Straight, knocked him over the head with a gun. As Holohan fell to the floor, Straight continued to savagely beat him. Mark Noon, the board secretary, was then forced to call for a car. The members of the board and the four convicts, taking two guards with them, drove off.

After a 25 mile chase, Noon and one of the guards were tossed out of the car. The rest of the group continued until they reached a barn. There, a shoot-out occurred with Straight being killed and two of the board members injured. Alexander MacKay and Joe Kristy were executed for their part in the escape. Fred Landers pled guilty, turned state's evidence, and was sentenced to life imprisonment.

No. 50005
Alexander MacKay

Into The Modern Era

As early as 1904, the idea that prisoners should be separated by type of crime, number of convictions, and consideration for the age of the offender were advocated. It was Warden Hoyle who worked out a plan to divide inmates into three groups. Each was completely segregated from the others and each had its own distinct uniform.

At the end of the 1930's, the policies developed by men like John Hoyle and James Johnston were finally implemented. By the time Clinton Duffy became warden, a detailed and systematic segregation of inmates was put into operation. The school which James Johnston encouraged had grown. Originally the prison chaplain was the only teacher. By the 1940's there was a full-time teaching staff which also drew instructors from local universities. During the Duffy era, the academic teaching program expanded to include vocational and trade facilities.

The Prison Library.

A Sign hanging in the Furniture Factory.

The Furniture Factory, 1940's.

Over 7,500,000 ration books were processed and mailed in record time during WW II.

Two events mark the Duffy era. The first was World War II. The second was creation of the California Department of Corrections, a central administrative organization for the state's prisons.

After the attack on Pearl Harbor, San Quentin facilities switched over to the production of needed war supplies. The jute mill changed over to making gunny sacks for use as sand

Assembling submarine nets for the Navy during WW II.

bags. Air raid sirens, submarine nets, ship fenders, cargo nets, first aid kits, cargo slings, and transport bunks were manufactured. The inmates also made scows and did the laundry for the Navy. They made shoe repairs for the armed forces. They equipped emergency supply kits for the Red Cross and processed and mailed 7,500,00 ration books.

The same patriotic feeling which held the nation together was also at work in San Quentin. Prisoners were

Processing raw jute for spinning into cords which would be woven into gunny sacks for useage as sand bags.

47

The San Quentin dance orchestra, "As Time Goes By" performed on network radio.

permitted to apply for parole to the armed services. They were trained at San Quentin to be welders, ship-fitters, and cooks. The inmates donated almost 3,000 pints of blood, bought hundreds of thousands of dollars in war bonds, and donated thousands of books to the military. It was truly an extraordinary effort.

It was also during this time that a radio program called "San Quentin on the Air" was produced. This nationwide network broadcast aired every Tuesday at 7:30 p.m. It featured a short talk by Warden Duffy, followed with such entertainment as music by the San Quentin orchestra aptly named, "As Time Goes By," led by John Hendricks. Sometimes the Glee Club would also sing. All of the talent was provided by the inmates at the prison.

The San Quentin inmate band as it appeared in the late 1930's.

Making bread for dinner in the Prison Bakery.

The Hobby Shop, which is still in operation today, was begun during Duffy's tenure. Many of the inmates are excellent artists and craftsman. Today, the inmates crafts are for sale at the Hobby Shop store outside of the prison's East Gate.

The establishment of the Department of Corrections organized the state prison system as we know it today. Prison jobs now came under civil service jurisdiction, no longer as political payoffs. A three person board, "The Adult Authority," would determine paroles and set the terms under the indeterminate sentence law. Richard A. McGee was appointed the first director of the Department of Corrections. It was under his leadership that the state correctional system grew into its present form.

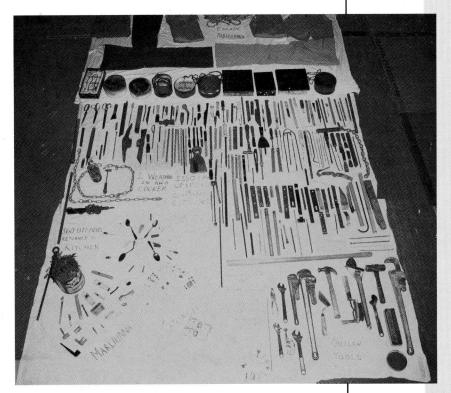

A new version of the ball and chain. A support device is attached to the convicts shoe, then a 30 lb. weight is fitted around his ankle. This was often used when a prisoner was being transported.

These weapons and contraband were seized from inmates between June 1 and June 30, 1977.

49

Pictures of Home

This is San Quentin? Home, for the employees working at San Quentin, is comfortable and very much like any suburban neighborhood in America.

Over the years, San Quentin has been home to hundreds of thousands of inmates and several thousand employees with family and children. While massive cell blocks may be the general image of San Quentin, it is also a place of beautiful tree lined streets with neat modest homes. A place with the sounds of children playing and lemonade stands on immaculate lawns on hot days.

A five man cell in the old Spanish block. These cells are no longer in use.

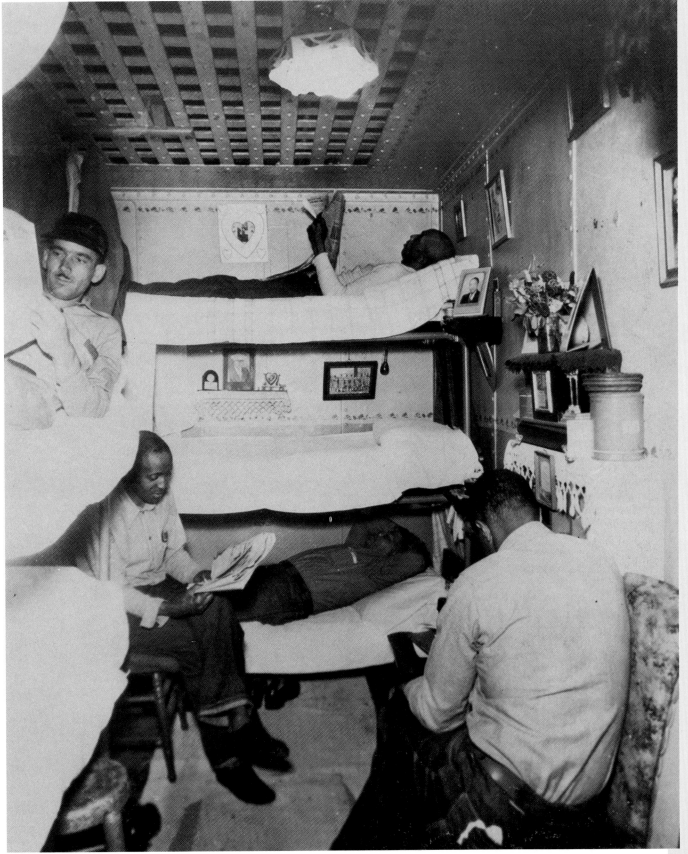

The picture above gives a somewhat "Southern California Resort" appearance. It is a view from the front of the old warden's residence, 1920's.

Left to top right: Nell, Muriel and Fulton, the children of Warden Johnston at home in San Quentin, 1920's.

Once there were farms operated by the prison. Hog farms to raise food for consumption by the inmates and a dairy for milk production, located on the hill in the picture above. Also, there was a large vegetable garden that supplied fresh produce. In the picture below, the row of houses in the background were for staff housing. The farms and gardens are now long gone.

The children of employees that lived on the prison grounds attended school in their own school house, which was built in 1924. It was a forerunner to the children in the workplace concept now so popular.

Today, parents with children on the premises say they feel their kids are absolutely safe. In case of illness or injury they can be contacted immediately. The school house on the prison property is no longer in use and the children are now taken by bus to the local community school.

Inmates who became ill were treated at the prison hospital. Now they are taken to local hospital facilities. When inmates died and their bodies were not claimed they were buried on Cemetary Hill. The graves were badly vandalized in the late 1960's but many of the markers have been salvaged and the graves identified. There are plans for restoration of the cemetary in the future.

For most of the inmates who live here, this is not a home by choice. There isn't a single inmate who does not long to be out. For them, a prison will always be just that, a prison.

In the late 1960's, these homes were used by the visiting families of inmates.

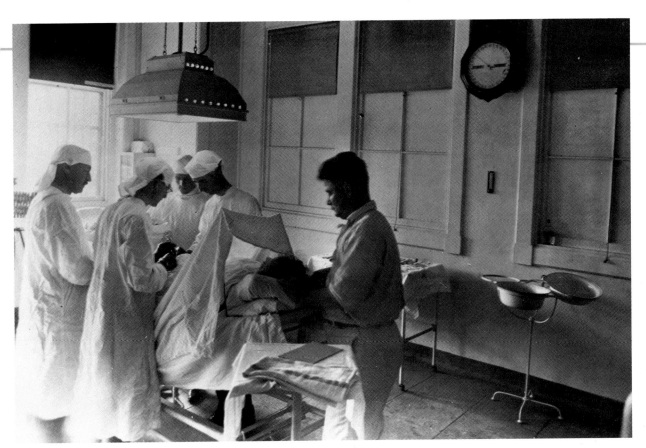

Dr. Stanley at work in 1934. He wrote, "The number of men who come to the hospital each day will average about 400, but at times, when there has been an epidemic of influenza or some other disease, there have been as many as 1100. Every man who comes to the prison is given a thorough examination . . . malingering just does not exist in this institution." At the time of 400 patients a day average the prison population was about 4,000. Today, 10% of the total being out ill at any given time is still considered "normal."

The gym for inmates which opened in 1967.

"Q" Today

by R. A. Nelson, Associate Warden

San Quentin Prison – "Q"

People at San Quentin fall into two groups – those who choose to be there and those who, on the whole, would rather not be there. The group that prefers not to be there, the inmates, are all convicted felons. As a rule of thumb, to be sentenced to a state prison an individual has committed a crime that received more than a one year's sentence. Today, with over-crowded prisons and backlogged court calendars, being sentenced to a state prison is not that easy. In 1990, only 1 out of 10 arrests went to trial. Only 15% of those convicted of a felony were actually sentenced to serve time in a state prison.

Over the years, San Quentin has held many types of inmates classified with different security levels. San Quentin, often referred to as " Q", has housed the most violent and dangerous of California's convicted felons. It is still the only prison designated to house Death Row inmates (male only). All state executions, including female prisoners, are conducted behind the walls of San Quentin.

Strip Search

Currently, San Quentin functions as the Northern California Reception Center and also houses inmates classified to a level II security institution (level IV being the highest).

The county, in which a person is convicted of his crime, transports him to San Quentin, (today, all inmates housed in San Quentin are men). The inmate is now turned over to the California Department of Corrections to serve his sentence. An inmate does not necessarily serve his entire sentence at any given institution. They are housed and moved from time to time for various reasons ranging from security concerns to space availability.

The following is a detailed chronology of what happens to a person after they have been convicted of a felony. Once a Judge has pronounced sentence the convicted felon is returned to the County Jail. He will await the preparation of the court documents commiting him to state prison. Also, he awaits transportation to the designated state prison reception center for

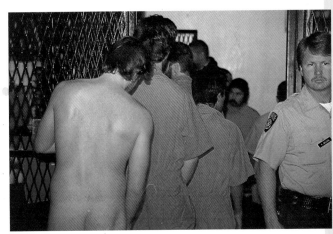

New Fish

the county of conviction. San Quentin is the Northern California Reception Center and accepts new commitments for the surrounding counties.

Upon arrival at "Q", an inmate is stripped of all clothes and possessions. He is given a bright orange jumpsuit and his legal paperwork, the rest of his personal possessions must either be sent out of the institution or donated. The new arrival, known as a "Fish," because

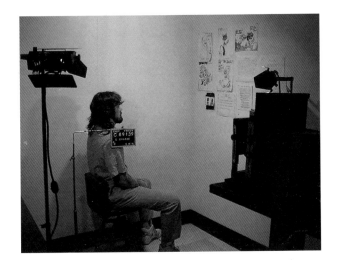

The Fish is Photographed.

West Block

Rows of cells for new inmates.

"Each inmate is given his state issue of toilet paper, comb, linens, towel, soap, toothbrush and blanket".

he has just been caught, is fingerprinted, I.D.'d, given his state issue of toilet paper, comb, linens, towel, soap, toothbrush, and blanket. He is then assigned a cell. These new arrivals are maintained under strict security until the staff has received the information on the inmates background.

Under escort these inmates are lead to West Block where all new commitments are housed two to a cell. For the next two weeks they undergo medical and physical examinations, I.Q. and Educational Testing and Staff Evaluation. These new arrivals are kept locked up approximately 23 hours a day and given yard priviledges twice a week for four hours. They are allowed no personal property and outside visitors are limited during this time. They are given restricted canteen priviledges in order to purchase additional personal items, including tobacco and stationery. After about two weeks, they are rehoused in different cell blocks depending upon staff evaluation, security level and space availability.

Inmates receive their blankets.

The next step causes the most concern to the inmates. The classification interview and endorsement recommendation. This interview will determine the inmates security level and at which prison he will most likely spend, at least, the next year.

Security Levels are determined by a classification score. The score is a numerical evaluation of an inmates personal and prior prison history. Taken into account is the length of the sentence and the type of crime committed and medical and psychiatric needs. Once a score is determined, a Correctional Counselor and the inmate confer on the available prisons in their security level. Two choices are made for housing the inmate. The interview results, the classification score, and the Counselors report are presented to the C.S.R. Board (Classification Score Review). The board makes the final determination where an inmate will be placed.

Inmates dressed in "blues".

Even if an inmate is assigned to San Quentin, he will wait for a bed assignment. When a space is made available, at San Quentin or another prison, the inmate is moved and placed in the "mainline." These inmates are usually dressed in "blues," all pants, shirts and jackets are blue.

Wall Mural at the Adjustment Center.

Most inmates participate in the Work Incentive Program. They can earn credit towards an earlier release date and benefits accorded a higher priviledge group. Jobs within San Quentin vary from Block Workers, Inmate Clerks, Maintenance Workers to Teachers Aids and Workers in the Industries Programs.

A Wall Mural in the Mess Hall depicts life outside of "Q".

The Mess Hall is considered the most dangerous place for both officers and inmates.

Some volunteer organizations provide services to the inmates such as Toastmasters, the Salvation Army, the Vietnam Veterans of America, Alchoholics Anonymous, Squires, Narcotics Anonymous, athletic organizations, and others working through the Community Resources Department and the Arts-In-Correction program.

Inmates at San Quentin are offered a wide variety of activities ranging from hobbycrafts and juggling to music and art classes. Also provided are educational classes in everything from G.E.D. to Computers.

Mass was held in the North Mess Hall

Exercise Yard

Inmates who have not earned an A-1 priviledge group are restricted to the upper yard and limited activities. Those with A-1 status are allowed to participate in all activities including recreation in the lower yard. The lower yard offers weight piles, softball fields and basketball courts. All inmates are allowed canteen priviledges but their limit is determined by status. Monthly spending is from $35 to $140. San Quentin offers a variety of religious activities in many faiths - church service, training and Bible studies.

The next step for an inmate endorsed to San Quentin Main Level II is to be moved into North Block. Here he awaits another classification known as U.C.C. (Unit Classification Committee). This review will determine the inmates housing, work, and priviledge group status. The inmates next step is to "program" or develop a routine. A program helps the inmate to keep on a schedule and pass time until he is eligible for transfer to a lower security institution or released.

A creative writing class being taught.

The other group of people at San Quentin? These are the individuals who have chosen to work at San Quentin. They are mostly staff personnel ranging from Correctional Officers to Educational Instructors, Correctional Counselors, Secretaries, Maintenance Workers, Medical Technicians and Doctors. There are Clergy representatives and Food Service people. Also, with great appreciation, there is a large group of volunteers at San Quentin.

Working at "Q" . . . Fifty-five percent of the employees are Correctional Officers. The current requirements for this position are: 21 years of age, hold a High School diploma, two years of Military experience or college and no felony convictions.

A potential officer candidate can make application to the California Department of Corrections. If the applicant is accepted he/she will go through a 6 week basic training session at the Department of Corrections Academy near Sacramento. This is an extensive course in search/seizure, basic laws of arrest, firearms training, drug identification, crime scene investigation, evidence preservation, institutional sanitation, fire/life safety, first aid, report writing and working with people under restraints. This is a California Police Officers Training Standards (POST) accredited course. After successful completion of the Academy the Officer begins the hands on training at an assigned institution.

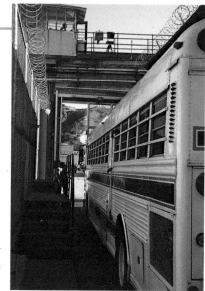

Department of Corrections transport bus.

Entrance through which the transport bus brings new inmates.

Just Visiting . . . today, anyone wishing to visit San Quentin will be run through the computers to check for prior felony convictions, wants and warrants. This includes inmate visitors as well as possible staff and volunteers. Guidelines for entering the prison are very strict for security reasons. Any person wishing to visit an inmate must submit a request in writing and wait for written approval before coming for a visit. Volunteers are handled on an individual basis through their service organizations.

Correctional Officers

Daniel Vasquez
Warden, San Quentin State Prison

In July of 1991 San Quentin was 139 years old. As Warden, the impact of this reality has been underscored for me by two significant personal experiences.

First and foremost, the significance of meeting many individuals who worked and retired from San Quentin years before I was even born. One memorable person, with whom I became friends, was the late Correctional Captain C. L. (Clarence) Doosey. Before his death, we spent some quality time together reminiscing about San Quentin of the past. Captain Doosey was a fascinating man who taught me a lot.

The second experience was the discovery of a historical time line. This was located on a wall in an area of the institution first used to store many artifacts from earlier days. The historical significance of this time line is that it illustrates San Quentin had already been in existence for a decade before Abraham Lincoln was first elected president of the United States. San Quentin participated in the course of early American history and has been in continuous operation to present day.

On a more personal level, I am approaching my 8th anniversary as the Warden of San Quentin. I am the 29th Warden to serve in the history of this noble prison. I and only 28 other people can claim the honor and human experience of such an assignment.

I may very well be the last Warden to administer at San Quentin during its history as a maximum security prison. Under the former mission of maximum custody, the prison population reached 1,750 inmates requiring the highest level of security; the largest such mission in the nation. This mission lasted 5-1/2 years during my watch as Warden. With the exception of Death Row, which remains at San Quentin, the former maximum custody mission has been shifted to newly constructed state-of-the-art maximum security prisons located in remote areas of California. The Gothic style of prisons like San Quentin will no longer be built. San Quentin, the prison itself, is only steel and concrete. The real San Quentin Prison is known through the stories of people and human drama that have unfolded for a continuous 139 years.

While it is true there are stories of violence and death at San Quentin, there are more important stories about the people who have served with dedication, sacrifice and courage. It is to these individuals and those who lost their lives in service to their fellow citizens, the story of "San Quentin - Inside the Walls," is dedicated.

VAGABOND THOUGHTS

MY THOUGHTS, as ragged vagabonds, roam
Down burly pathways I once have known.
Up through the air, on land, at sea;
Regardless of me, they remain free.
Recalling a snatch of song that thrills,
The touch of a hand, or word that fills
My exiled heart with longing to be
As heedless as they are gay and carefree.
Then the droning sounds of the old hall clock
Announce it is time for the doors to lock.

Alone the setting sun beckons to me –
Vagabonds thoughts answer – for they are free.

– Inmate Velma Williams, 1936.